300
WITZE

Jörg Schötensack

300 WITZE
FÜRS SPRACHTRAINING

Inhalt

Vorwort

Bevor der Spaß beginnt

Lächerlich leicht Englisch lernen? Das soll gehen? Natürlich, und zwar im positiven Sinn des Wortes "lächerlich", nämlich anhand von dreihundert Witzen, die wir für Sie ausgesucht und in diesem Buch gesammelt haben.

Beim Lesen der Witze sollen Sie nicht nur ordentlich lachen, sondern gleichzeitig die Möglichkeit haben, Ihren Umgang mit Englisch zu verbessern. Damit das auch klappt und um Ihnen das Lernen zu erleichtern, machen wir Sie als erstes ganz knapp mit einigen ausgewählten Grammatikregeln vertraut, auf die man leider beim Lernen einer Sprache nicht ganz verzichten kann, denn es ist ja bekanntlich noch kein Meister vom Himmel gefallen. Aber keine Angst: Es sind nicht so viele Regeln, dass Ihnen gleich wieder der Spaß vergeht und das Lachen im Halse stecken bleibt!

Den Gebrauch der Zeiten ausgenommen, ist jede Grammatikregel mit einem Symbol versehen, und die jeweiligen Symbole finden Sie bei den Witzen wieder. Das, worauf sich das Symbol bei einem Witz bezieht, worauf es also ankommt, haben wir kursiv gesetzt: Dort kommt die Regel zum Tragen, und dort sollten Sie bezüglich ihrer Verwendung aufmerksam hinschauen – natürlich erst nachdem Sie über den Witz gelacht haben.
Der Übersichtlichkeit halber haben wir uns hier darauf beschränkt, pro Witz auf eine Grammatikregel aufmerksam zu machen. Auch aus Gründen der Übersichtlichkeit haben

wir die Zeiten zwar erklärt, aber nicht extra markiert, denn Sie werden sie selber problemlos erkennen können. So können Sie sich den Witzen hingeben und notfalls, wenn etwas unklar erscheint, schnell einmal im Grammatikteil die Regel unter dem entsprechenden Symbol nachschlagen oder sich vergewissern, wie die Zeiten richtig gebraucht werden. Wörter, deren Bedeutung sie vielleicht noch nicht kennen, haben wir direkt unter den jeweiligen Witzen erklärt, um Ihnen das lästige Nachschlagen zu ersparen. Es kommt vor, dass die gleichen Wörter innerhalb verschiedener Witze mehrmals auftauchen, so dass Sie das Buch einfach irgendwo aufschlagen können, um darin zu schmökern. Die Witze selber sind nach Themen gegliedert, die so ziemlich alles abdecken, was interessant ist, und zwar:

- Familie und Alltag
- Tiere
- Berufe
- Arbeit
- Essen
- Freizeit und Diverses

Und als kleines Extra, das Sie sicher ebenfalls interessieren wird, finden Sie am unteren Rand der Seiten über hundert Redewendungen „am laufenden Band" mit ihren deutschen Entsprechungen, sodass Sie, auch was „Idioms" angeht, künftig als „Insider" mitreden können.

Nun aber ran ans Vergnügen!

Enjoy yourselves and have a good laugh!

Ausgewählte Grammatik

 Tempora – *Tenses*

Konditionalsätze – *If-clauses*

Fragesätze – *Questions*

Adjektive und Adverbien – *Adjectives and Adverbs*

Präpositionen – *Prepositions*

Unbestimmte Zahlwörter bzw. Mengenbezeichnungen – *Indefinite Quantifiers*

 **Tempora** – *Tenses*

Es gibt im Englischen acht Zeiten. Für jede geben wir ein Beispiel anhand eines Verbs in der ersten Form Singular, damit Sie wissen, was sich dahinter verbirgt. Einen Gesamtüberblick kann dieses Buch leider nicht geben. Für diesen Zweck sollten Sie eine umfassende Grammatik zur Hand nehmen. Dort finden Sie auch weiterführende, wichtige Informationen, wie beispielsweise zum Gebrauch von unregelmäßigen Verben. Um Sie nicht mit zu vielen Symbolen zu bombardieren, haben wir, wie bereits in der Einleitung erwähnt, den Gebrauch der Zeiten dort nicht extra ausgezeichnet. Es wird Ihnen sicher nicht schwer fallen, die Zeiten selbst zu erkennen.

Präsens/Gegenwart (*Present Tense*)

II watch (*simple*)
I am watching (*continuous*)

Imperfekt bzw. Präteritum/Vergangenheit (*Past Tense*)

I watched (*simple*)
I was watching (*continuous*)

Perfekt/Vollendete Gegenwart (*Present Perfect*)

I have watched (*simple*)
I have been watching (*continuous*)

Plusquamperfekt/Vorvergangenheit (*Past Perfect*)

I had watched (*simple*)
I had been watching (*continuous*)

Futur I/Zukunft I (*Future I*)

I will watch (*simple*)
I will be watching (*continuous*)

Futur II/Zukunft II (*Future II*)

I will have watched (*simple*)
I will have been watching (*continuous*)

Konditional I (*Conditional I*)

I would watch (*simple*)
I would be watching (*continuous*)

Konditional II (*Conditional II*)

I would have watched (*simple*)
I would have been watching (*continuous*)

# Konditionalsätze – *If-clauses*

Konditionalsätze drücken typischerweise eine Bedingung aus. Im Englischen gibt es davon drei Grundtypen, und jeder funktioniert nach einer bestimmten Regel bezüglich der Zeitenfolge. Insofern sind Konditionalsätze eng mit dem Gebrauch der Zeiten verknüpft.

Hier sind nun die Kurzregeln der drei Grundtypen. Aber: Vorsicht! Jede dieser Regeln kann nach bestimmten Gesetzmäßigkeiten, jedoch unter der Berücksichtigung der Zeiten, erweitert werden. Hierfür schauen Sie am besten in ein Grammatikbuch!

Wahrscheinliche Bedingung (*Probable Condition*)

If I laugh (*Present Tense*), I will be in a good mood (*Future I*)

Unwahrscheinliche Bedingung (*Improbable Condition*)

If I laughed (*Past Tense*), I would be in a good mood (*Conditional I*)

Unmögliche Bedingung (*Impossible Condition*)

If I had laughed (*Past Perfect*), I would have been in a good mood (*Conditional II*)

❓ Fragesätze – *Questions*

Fragesätze können natürlich leicht am Fragezeichen am Ende des Satzes erkannt werden. Sie können im Englischen auf drei verschiedene Arten geformt werden:

mit Fragewörtern wie z. B. *what* (What time is it?), *who* (Who is he?), *which* (Which one do you mean?), *why* (Why are you shy?), *when* (When are we going?), *where* (Where do you live?), *how* (How much does it cost?)

mit dem Hilfsverb *do* (Do you like it? Does he work here? Did you go there?)

mit den folgenden Hilfsverben:
am (Am I late?), *are* (Are you married?), *is* (Is it real?), *was* (Was he here?), *were* (Were you mad at me?)
can (Can I help you?), *could* (Could you do me a favour?)
have (Have you been there?), *has* (Has he called you?), *had* (Had he warned you?)
may (May I talk to you?), *might* (Might Mr. Smith have it, perhaps?)
must (Must I go to bed?)
need (Need I say more?)
shall (Shall I introduce you?), *should* (Should we see the movie?)
will (Will you marry me?), *would* (Would you come tomorrow?)

Adjektive und Adverbien – *Adjectives and Adverbs*

Adjektive und Adverbien sind im Englischen ein weites Feld, wir können uns hier nur auf das Wesentliche beschränken. Auch bei der Kennzeichnung innerhalb der Witze haben wir uns auf diejenigen Adjektive und Adverbien beschränkt, die am deutlichsten für sich stehen.

Adjektive bezeichnen eine Eigenschaft und sind nach Numerus, Genus und Kasus nicht veränderlich. Die meisten kurzen Adjektive sind jedoch insofern veränderlich, als sie gesteigert werden können (z. B. *nice, nicer, nicest*). Längere Adjektive werden in der Regel mit more und most gesteigert (z. B. *interesting, more interesting, most interesting*).

Adjektive können in Vergleichssätzen u. a. mit *as ... as* (z. B. *as interesting as*) und *less ... than* (z. B. *less interesting than*) auftreten.

Adverbien bezeichnen einen Umstand. Es gibt zwei Arten: Die ursprünglichen (z. B. *here, there, now*) und die von Adjektiven abgeleiteten (z. B. *nicely*). Den von Adjektiven abgeleiteten Adverbien wird in vielen Fällen einfach nur ein "*-ly*" angehängt (z. B. *common* wird zu *commonly*).

Adverbien können ebenfalls gesteigert werden und folgen dabei meist einem gleichen Schema (z. B. *late, later, latest*). Auf "*-ly*" endende Adverbien werden mit *more* und *most* gesteigert (z. B. *cleverly, more cleverly, most cleverly*).

Präpositionen – *Prepositions*

Präpositionen sind Verhältniswörter, die sich in fünf
Hauptgruppen unterteilen lassen:
Raum (z. B. *on, in front of*)
Zeit (z. B. *during, before*)
Art und Weise (z. B. *with, by means of*)
Zweck, Absicht (z. B. *for, in order to*)
Ursache, Grund (z. B. *due to, because of*)

Die gebräuchlichsten Präpositionen sind
at, in, on (in räumlicher oder zeitlicher Bedeutung)
above, over, across, via – über
under, below – unter
between, among – zwischen
to, towards – zu(m)
to, as far as – bis
after, behind, beyond, past – hinter
in front of, before – vor
ago, before – vor (nachgestellt)
since, for – seit
by, with – mit

Präpositionen treten übrigens oft in Verbindung mit Verben
auf, so beispielsweise bei *to agree with* (übereinstimmen
mit), *to complain about* (sich beschweren über) oder *to give
up* (aufgeben).

Unbestimmte Zahlwörter bzw. Mengen-
bezeichnungen – *Indefinite Quantifiers*

Weil sie häufig fehlerhaft verwendet werden, haben wir die unbestimmten Zahlwörter beziehungsweise Mengenbezeichnungen ebenfalls mit aufgenommen. Hierzu gehören u. a. *some* und *any*, *much* und *many* und *little* und *few*.

Some/any

Some wird in bejahenden Sätzen gebraucht (z. B. *There is some coffee in the kitchen*). Es findet sich in Fragesätzen, auf die eine bejahende Antwort erwartet wird (z. B. *Would you like some coffee?*), und in Fragesätzen, die mit Fragewörtern wie beispielsweise *where, when, how* eingeleitet werden (z. B. *Where can I get some coffee?*).
Any steht dagegen im verneinenden Satz (z. B. *There isn't any coffee in the kitchen*) sowie im Fragesatz (z. B. *Is there any coffee in the kitchen?*). Und verneint Nebensätze von Konditionalsätzen (z. B. *If there was any coffee, I would drink it*).

Much/many und little/few

Much und *many* werden ebenfalls größtenteils in verneinenden Sätzen und in Fragen gebraucht (z. B. *There isn't much coffee left* bzw. *Have you got many guests?*).
Much und *little* kennzeichnen nicht zählbare Begriffe (z. B. *There isn't much coffee left* bzw. *There is only a little sugar left*).
Many und *few* stehen vor zählbaren Begriffen (z. B. *There aren't many cups left* bzw. *There are only a few cups left*).

Die Witze

Familie und Alltag

A woman said to her husband, "We should buy junior a bike."
The father said, "Will that make him behave *better*?"
The woman said, "I don't think so, but it'll spread his bad behaviour over a *bigger* area!"

behaviour	**Benehmen, Betragen, Verhalten**
to spread	**ausbreiten, verteilen**

The new baby was crying *in* his crib as his five-year-old brother watched him. The five-year-old asked his mother as she comforted the baby, "Where did we get him?"
The mother said, "He came *from* heaven."
The baby screamed again and the five-year-old said, "I can see why they threw him *out*!"

crib	**Krippe**
to comfort	**trösten**
heaven	**Himmel**

It's a dog's life – Es ist ein Hundeleben

In the middle of their *worst* quarrel of the day, the husband decided to take a walk. After an hour he was *calmer* and called the house. "Honey, what are you making for dinner?"

His wife answered, "Poison!"

"Make only *enough* for one. I'm eating out!"

quarrel	Streit
calm	ruhig
poison	Gift

Jenny watched her mother put cream on her face and asked, "*What's* that cream for?"

The mother said, "It's facial cream to make me look gorgeous."

A few minutes later, the mother removed the cream. Jenny stared and then said, "It *didn't* work, did it?"

facial cream	Gesichtscreme
gorgeous	hinreißend, herrlich, großartig

Hope springs eternal – Wenn die Hoffnung nicht wäre

Two youngsters are left alone by their mother, who has to run to the supermarket for a few moments. The older child, a girl of seven, is left in charge. She'll be the mother until the real one returns. Bugged, the five-year-old son says to his sister, "Okay, if you're the mummy, how *many* apples are three times six?"

The sister replies, "Wait until your father comes home!"

youngster	**Kind**
in charge	**verantwortlich**
bugged	**genervt, verstört**

He looked *at* his family tree, and they were still living *in* it!

family tree	**Stammbaum (Wortspiel!)**

Two men were talking about life when the subject started to focus on the family. One man said, "I met my wife at a dance." The other man said, "That's *nice*."

The first one said, "I don't know. I thought she was at home taking care of the kids!"

To see pink elephants – Weiße Mäuse sehen

"Dad, *does* ink cost a lot of money?"

"No. *Why*?"

"Mum wanted to kill me because I spilled some on her new carpet!"

ink	**Tinte**
to spill	**verschütten**
carpet	**Teppich**

Hit or miss – Auf gut Glück

A woman is well into her pregnancy, as is obvious from her roundness. Wishing to involve her six-year-old son, she asks, "What would you rather have - a boy or a girl?"
The boy says, "*If* it doesn't get you out of shape too much, I'll have a pony!"

pregnancy	Schwangerschaft
obvious	offensichtlich, deutlich
to involve	einbeziehen

"My family records go back ten centuries. *How* about yours?"
"They were lost in the Flood!"

century	Jahrhundert
the Flood	die Sintflut

Nurse: "Sir, you've just become the father of lovely twins."
Man: "Don't tell my wife. I want to surprise her!"

nurse	Krankenschwester

To go the whole hog – Aufs Ganze gehen

An eight-year-old child hadn't said one word in his entire life. One day, however, as the family sat down to have breakfast, the boy asked, "*Do* we have any jam?"
The family was stunned. When they'd recovered, the father said, "*How* come you never said one word before?"
The boy said, "Well, up to now, everything has been okay!"

entire	**ganz**
stunned	**fassungslos, sprachlos**
to recover	**sich erholen, wieder zu sich kommen**

"Daddy, I can't find the *greatest* common divisor."
"Are they still looking for that? They couldn't find it at the time when I was a child either!"

As part of spring cleaning, they threw out *a lot of* useless things. They started with *some* of their relatives!

spring cleaning	**Frühjahrsputz**

Not to be able to hold a candle to someone
Jemandem nicht das Wasser reichen können

A busy executive received a phone call *from* a nurse *at* the hospital. The nurse informed him that he was the father *of* a fine young son. The executive answered, "Why call me *about* it? My wife always takes care *of* those matters!"

executive   **leitender Angestellter**

"*Is* there a way to avoid alimony?"
"Of course, stay single or stay married!"

alimony   **Unterhaltszahlung**

The father was slightly annoyed when he said to his inquisitive son, "You never stop asking questions. All day long you ask questions. Where would I be *if* I asked questions like you?"
The son answered, "You might be able to answer some of mine!"

slightly   **ein wenig**
annoyed   **verärgert**

Go to hell – Scher dich zum Teufel

On the eve of their twentieth wedding anniversary Mrs. Smith asks, "*Don't* you think we should do something?"
"I certainly do," Mr. Smith replies.
"*How* do you suggest we should celebrate it?"
"*How* about two minutes of silence?"

wedding anniversary	**Hochzeitstag**
to suggest	**vorschlagen**
to celebrate	**feiern**
silence	**Schweigen, Stille**

The psychiatrist examined ten-year-old Willie and told his mother, "Mrs. Miller, you need *some* help too. You're too concerned and nervous about your son. I'll give you *a few* tranquillizers that you'll take regularly until I see you next week."
The following week, the Millers returned. The psychiatrist asked, "How's Willie?"
Mrs. Miller said, "Who cares?"

psychiatrist	**Psychiater**
to examine	**untersuchen**
concerned	**besorgt**
tranquillizer	**Beruhigungstablette**

To be head over heels in love
Bis über beide Ohren verliebt sein

A baby brightens *up* the home. Since ours came, the lights have been *on* all night!

to brighten up   **aufhellen, aufheitern**

A father asked the young man who had been seeing his daughter about his finances. "What will be your *yearly* income?" the father asked.
"Fifty thousand," the young man said.
"Not too *bad.* When you add my daughter's forty thousand, that'll be *decent* enough."
"Oh, I already counted her in the fifty!"

income   **Einkommen**
decent   **anständig**

A visiting aunt watched her niece learning to write. The aunt asked, "Where is the dot *over* the i?"
The niece answered, "It's still *in* the pen!"

niece   **Nichte**

A wet blanket – Ein Spielverderber

"My sister is going to have a baby."
"*Did* you call her up?"
"I don't have to. She knows about it!"

To be hand in glove with someone
Mit jemandem unter einer Decke stecken

A man is driving *with* his wife *at* his side and his mother-in-law in the backseat. The women don't leave him alone. His mother-in-law says, "You're driving too fast!"
His wife says, "Stay more *to* the left!"
After ten mixed orders, the man *turns to* his wife and asks, "Who's driving this car - you or your mother?"

mother-in-law   **Schwiegermutter**

A husband ran out of the house and rushed off to the *nearest* bar. At two in the morning he called his wife and told her, "I'm coming home."
The wife said, "Well, you've *finally* decided that home is *best* after all."
The husband said, "Not *necessarily*, but it's the *only* place open at this hour!"

to rush off   **wegeilen, weghasten**

"*What* did your daughter do last summer?"
"Her hair and her nails!"

A bird in the hand is worth two in the bush
Der Spatz in der Hand ist besser als die Taube auf dem Dach

Two young prep school boys were *talking about* their ancestry. One said, "I can trace my family back to biblical days. My family was probably *on* the Ark *with* Noah." The other one retorted, "My family had a boat *of* its own!"

prep school	private Vorbereitungsschule
ancestry	Abstammung, Herkunft
to trace	zurückverfolgen
biblical	biblisch
the Ark	die Arche (Noah)
to retort	erwidern

A man of eighty smiles with happiness as the nurse enters and tells him that his twenty-year-old wife has just given birth to a small boy. The man muses, "I wonder *if* I could do it again."
Another expectant father answers, "What makes you think you did it the first time?"

nurse	Krankenschwester
wife	Ehefrau
to give birth	gebären
to muse	nachdenken
expectant	erwartungsvoll

The coast is clear – Die Luft ist rein

"*What's* the matter with your brother?"
"He lost his wife and he's going crazy."
"*Is* he going to get married again?"
"No, he's not that crazy!"

crazy	**verrückt**
to marry	**heiraten**

"Are you *still* engaged to that *ugly* Kramer girl?"
"No."
"What happened?"
"I married her!"

Parents spend the first *few* years of a child's life trying to get him to talk. They spend the rest trying to get the child to shut up!

People who have a baby can't sleep *like* one.

To give someone a piece of one's mind
Jemandem den Kopf waschen

Two grandmothers, wheeling their grandchildren in *fancy* prams, met in the park. One admired the baby in the *pink-frilled* pram. *Naturally*, the *other* grandmother had to repay the compliment and admired the two in the *larger* pram. She asked how *old* those *beautiful* babies were. The *proud* grandmother said, "The doctor is eight months old. The judge is a year and a half."

fancy	schick, ausgefallen
pram	Kinderwagen
to admire	bewundern
pink-frilled	mit rosafarbenen Rüschen
proud	stolz
judge	Richter

"*Is* your husband hard to please?"
"I don't know. I've never tried!"

Dog's breakfast – Schlamassel

Mrs. Carter answered the phone to hear an anguished voice *on* the other end *of* the line saying, "Mum, this has been the worst day *of* my life. I'm going crazy. The children are all sick and home *from* school. I haven't a thing *in* the house. I have a doctor's appointment. I'm going *out of* my mind!"

"I'll come over," Mrs. Carter said, "but I don't know why Victor can't *take care of* the children."

"Who's Victor?"

"Your husband."

"My husband's name is Alan."

"You must have the wrong number."

"Oh, does that mean you're not coming *over*?"

anguished	**qualvoll**
appointment	**Termin**

The *new* bride told her mother, "My husband is *very good* to me. He gives me everything I ask for."

The mother said, "That *merely* shows you're not asking *enough*."

merely	**lediglich**
bride	**Braut**

To make a killing – Einen Riesengewinn machen

A man offered his wife a fortune in alimony *if* she'd give him a divorce. She refused, saying, "After all these years, why should I make him happy?"

a fortune	ein Vermögen
alimony	Unterhaltszahlung
divorce	Scheidung

Divorce is the future tense *of* marriage.

The baby, a girl, was born two days *later* than expected. Holding her, her father said, "Two minutes *old* and she's *already* kept a man waiting!"

to expect	erwarten

"That's a nice coat. *Did* your husband change jobs?"
"No, I changed husbands!"

You can't make a silk purse out of a sow's ear
Aus nichts wird nichts

A wife said *to* her husband, "Let's not stay *at* home all the time. Let's go *out* three times a week."
The husband said, "Good idea. You *go out on* Monday, Wednesday, and Friday!"

A *young* lady came home from a date, *rather sad*. She told her mother, "Robert proposed to me an hour ago."
"Why are you *so sad*?" her mother asked.
"Because he *also* told me he was an atheist. Mother, he doesn't even believe there is a hell."
Her mother said, "Marry him anyway. Between the two of us, we'll show him *how wrong* he is!"

to propose   **vorschlagen,**
                   einen Heiratsantrag machen

This man's daughter broke up with her boyfriend. She sent back his sweets and *some* books of poetry, but kept the jewelry for sentimental reasons.

book of poetry   **Gedichtbuch**

To have a crush on someone – In jemanden verliebt sein

She's a housekeeper. *Every* time she gets divorced, she keeps the house.

housekeeper	**Haushälterin (Wortspiel!)**
divorced	**geschieden**

A man was telling *of* his power at home, saying, "I'm the boss at home. Just this morning there was no hot water. I was furious. I demanded hot water and got hot water. I can't wash dishes *in* cold water!"

power	**Macht**
furious	**wütend**
dishes	**Geschirr**

"My nurse used to drop me *frequently.*"
"What did your mother do?"
"She got me a *shorter* nurse!"

nurse	**Krankenschwester, hier Kinderfrau**

As ugly as sin – Hässlich wie die Nacht

A teenager came to his father and said, "Dad, don't you think it's time I stood on my own two feet?"
"I do."
"I have to face the world and handle my own problems."
"Of course."
"I must make my own way."
"That's right."
"Well, I can't do it on the *little* money I get now!"

Two *very rich* people got divorced, and their lawyers lived *happily ever after*!

divorced	**geschieden**
lawyer	**Rechtsanwalt**

A man took his wife to a psychiatrist and said, "What's-her-name *here* complains that I don't give her *enough* attention!"

psychiatrist	**Psychiater**
to complain	**sich beschweren**

To be hopping mad – Fuchsteufelswild sein

A couple were celebrating their twenty-fifth wedding anniversary with a lavish party at a fancy restaurant. Everybody was having a great time except the husband, who sat in a corner with a tear in his eye. The family lawyer came over to him and asked what was wrong. The husband said, "Remember when we were first married and I couldn't stand her? I hated her."

The lawyer said, "I recall those days."

"I hated her with every bone in my body. I wanted to kill her, remember?"

"I remember."

"You wouldn't let me. You said *if* I killed her, I'd get twenty-five years in prison for the crime."

"That was a long time ago. Why are you so sad?"

"Because today I would have been a free man!"

to celebrate	**feiern**
anniversary	**Jubiläum**
lavish	**großzügig, üppig**
fancy	**schick, ausgefallen**
bone	**Knochen**

Fortune favours fools
Manche haben mehr Glück als Verstand

No man knows *how* short a month can be until he has to pay alimony.

"Dad, *where* are the Himalayas?"
"Ask your mother. She puts everything away!"

Old Mr. Collins staggered into the house and told his *young* wife, "I'm going to fire that chauffeur. He *almost* killed me a dozen times."
The wife said, "Dear, let's not be *hasty*. Give him one *more* chance!"

to stagger	taumeln, schwanken
to fire	entlassen

An Eskimo mother was sitting in her igloo reading a bed-time story to her small son. „Little Jon McMellow sat in a corner ..." „Mum," interrupted the boy, „*what's* a corner?"

To bark up the wrong tree
Auf dem falschen Dampfer sitzen

A *beautiful* woman, known for her vanity, took her *young* daughter to a department store. While the mother tried on a dress, the daughter picked up a hat, put it on, and looked at herself in the mirror. "Mother," the daughter said. "Look. I'm as *beautiful* as you in this hat."
The mother said, "Don't be *vain*, dear!"

vanity   Eitelkeit

What is the world to a man, when his wife is a widow?

A woman wanted a divorce because she said her husband never *took* her *out*. He explained to the judge, "I never *go out with* married women!"

judge   Richter

A teenage girl said *to* her mother, "Don't yell *at* me. I'm not your husband!"

Alike as two peas in a pot
Sich gleichen wie ein Ei dem anderen

A woman went to her doctor and complained that her husband talked in his sleep. The doctor said, "I'll give you a mild sedative."
The woman said, "Give me a *little* something to stay awake. I don't want to miss a thing!"

| to complain | sich beschweren |
| sedative | Beruhigungsmittel |

The teacher asked, "How *many* of you children want to go to heaven?"
All but one boy raised their hands. He said, "I can't. I have to go home right after school."

The *ugliest* man in the world married the *ugliest* woman in the world. After a year they had a *beautiful* baby. The husband looked at his wife and said, "Where did we go *wrong*?"

| ugly | hässlich |
| to go wrong | etwas falsch machen |

To know which side your bread is buttered on
Zu wissen, wo der Barthel den Most holt

It takes two to make an engagement - a girl and her *anxious* mother.

engagement	**Verlobung**
anxious	**besorgt**

A fly in the ointment – Eine Fliege in der Suppe

Two women met while shopping. When they started to talk about their home lives, one of them said, "I've been fighting day and night with my husband. It's so aggravating, I've lost twenty pounds."
The other woman said, "Stop arguing."
The first woman said, "Not yet. I want to lose *some* more weight!"

aggravating	**ärgerlich**
to argue	**streiten**
weight	**Gewicht**

A young boy calls to his mother, "Mum, which would you rather have happen - *if* I fell off a tree or *if* I tore my trousers?"
The mother answers, "Of course I'd pray that you tore your trousers."
The boy says, "Your prayers have been answered!"

A husband was telling a friend, "*If* my wife really loved me, she would have married somebody else!"

To live in sin – In wilder Ehe leben

Tiere

"*Do* you think I'm going to wear this squirrel coat for the rest of my life?"
"*Why* not? The squirrel did!"

squirrel	Eichhörnchen

The early bird would never catch the worm *if* the dumb worm slept late.

A dog, the barber's pet, stared at the man whose hair was being cut. The man said to the barber, "That's a *funny* dog. He likes watching haircuts."
The barber said, "That's not it. You see, once in a while I snip off an ear."

pet	Haustier
barber	Friseur
haircut	Haarschnitt
to snip off	wegschnipseln

Teacher's pet – Lehrers Liebling

We have a neurotic canary. He *hangs* by his feet all day and thinks he's a bat!

neurotic	neurotisch
bat	Fledermaus

A mouse goes "Ruff, ruff!" and the cat runs away. The mother mouse says, "*Do* you see the advantage of a second language?"

advantage	Vorteil

Many of the world's greatest runners come from Kenya because they have a unique training programme there - it's called a lion!

To pull at someone's heartstrings
Jemanden zu Tränen rühren

"Will an alligator hurt you *if* you carry a torch?"
"It depends on how fast you carry the torch!"

torch	**Fackel, Taschenlampe**
to depend on	**abhängen von**

A man is walking his dog when it gets *away* from him and attacks a woman on a *nearby* lawn. She runs inside her house and sends out her husband. The dog owner is *truly* sorry. He says, "Sir, how about a settlement? Will twenty pounds do?"
The husband says, "Of course. And if you return *next* week, I'll give you thirty!"

nearby	**nahe**
owner	**Besitzer**
settlement	**Einigung**

A very clever man put his hand into a lion's mouth to see *if* the lion had any teeth. The lion closed his mouth to see *if* the man had any fingers!

Grin and bear it – Gute Miene zum bösen Spiel machen

A bear approached a trapper *in* the woods and asked what he was *looking for*.

"I'm *after* a nice fur coat *for* myself," the trapper said. "How about you?"

"I'd like a nice breakfast. I tell you what, let's go *into* the cave and discuss it."

They went *into* the bear's cave and everything worked out. *In* half an hour the bear had his breakfast and the trapper was *in* a nice fur coat!

to approach	auf etwas zugehen
fur coat	Pelzmantel
cave	Höhle

To be done up like a dog's dinner
Wie eine Fregatte aufgetakelt sein

"*What* can you do with alligator skins?"
"Keep alligators in them!"

Scientists say that animals laugh. How could they resist *if* they watched human beings act!

scientists	**Wissenschaftler**
to resist	**widerstehen**

Tortoises are helping science. Recently, the heart *of* a tortoise was put *into* a man. The man walked *out* of the hospital a week later, and six weeks later he reached his car!

tortoise	**Schildkröte**
recently	**vor kurzem**

Kill-joy – Spielverderber

Witze

A woman browsing through an antique store sees a cat drinking milk from a saucer. She recognizes the saucer as a rare antique piece. Trying to be clever, she says to the lady running the store, "How *much* do you want for the cat?"
The woman says, "Ten pounds."
The buyer goes on, "While I'm at it, could I give you another pound for the saucer? The cat seems to enjoy drinking from it."
The shopkeeper shakes her head. "Sorry, but I've sold nineteen cats from that one saucer!"

to browse	**sich umsehen**
saucer	**Untertasse**
to recognize	**erkennen**

"My neighbour's dog bit me in the leg today."
"*Did* you put anything on it?"
"No, he liked it just as it was."

Two fleas meet in the street. One says to the other, "*Do* you want to walk or catch a dog?"

To horse around – Rumalbern

A man called his stockbroker and said, "What do you think I ought to do about pork bellies?"
The broker said, "Diet and a *little* exercise!"

| stockbroker | Börsenmakler |
| pork bellies | Schweinebäuche |

A rabbit and a lion went into a small restaurant. The rabbit ordered some lettuce and a carrot.
The waitress asked, "What will the lion have?"
The lion said, "Nothing. I'm not hungry."
The rabbit said, "*If* he was hungry, do you think I'd be here?"

| lettuce | Kopfsalat |
| waitress | Kellnerin |

A mother kangaroo complained to a friend, "I hate it when it's raining and the children have to play *inside*!"

| to complain | sich beschweren |

A king's ransom – Eine stolze Summe

A bear was just about to enter his winter's cave, but stopped *for* a moment *in order to* remind his friend, the woodpecker, "Remember, you have to wake me *at* half *past* April!"

cave	**Höhle**
woodpecker	**Specht**

The mother turkey said to her playboy son, "*If* your father saw you now, he'd turn over in his gravy!"

turkey	**Truthahn**
gravy	**Soße**
	(Wortspiel mit "grave" Grab!)

Animals can tell when an earthquake is on the way, and they try to get as fast as they can away from it. Just before the last earthquake we had, I saw a tortoise leading a rabbit by *many* lengths!

earthquake	**Erdbeben**

To have one over the eight – Einen über den Durst trinken

A man walked into a bar with a dog, claimed that the animal could talk, and offered to sell it. The barman refused to believe the claim and was going to blame it on the full moon when the dog said, "Buy me. Somebody please buy me. My owner is *mean* and *vicious*. He's *always* kicking me and hitting me. I happen to be a *great* dog. I was in the service. I have three medals for bravery. Please buy me." The barman asked the owner, "How can you sell such a *wonderful* dog?"
The man answered, "I'm *sick* and *tired* of his lies!"

to claim	behaupten
owner	Besitzer
mean	gemein
vicious	boshaft
the service	die Armee
medal	Orden
bravery	Tapferkeit

An ostrich arrived near the watering hole and saw all the other ostriches with their heads in the sand. Puzzled, the newly arrived ostrich says, "*Where* did everybody go?"

ostrich	Strauß

Strictly for the birds – Das ist geschenkt

Two goats were nibbling at the rubbish bin. One of them found and chewed up an old book. The other asked, "*Did you like that?*"
The chewer answered, "Actually I liked the film better!"

goat	**Ziege**
to nibble	**knabbern**
to chew	**kauen**

To get on like a house on fire – Gute Freunde sein

A young man bought an expensive parrot as a pet for his mother. When he visited her the following week, she invited him to dinner. On the table she put the parrot, roasted to perfection. The man jumped up. "Mum," he said, not believing his eyes, "that parrot cost a fortune. It spoke seven languages. How could you roast it?"
His mother answered indignantly, "*If* I spoke seven languages, I would have said something!"

parrot	**Papagei**
roasted	**gebraten**
a fortune	**ein Vermögen**
indignantly	**entrüstet**

A man walked into a bar and sat down. There didn't seem to be a barman. After a *few* moments, from the door at the back of the bar, a horse came out. Tying an apron around its waist, the horse asked the man if he wanted a drink. The man stared. The horse asked, "Why are you staring? Didn't you ever see a horse before?" The man answered, "Well, I didn't think the cow would sell the place!"

to tie	**binden**
apron	**Schürze**

Between you and me and the gatepost – Unter vier Augen

A snake went *to* a psychiatrist and claimed that all *of* his friends kept sticking out their tongues *at* him.

psychiatrist	Psychiater
to claim	behaupten

An impresario was interested in a dancing fly for his *new* show. A carnival man promised to deliver one. *Later* he apologized, "I couldn't train that fly to dance. He's got two *left* wings!"

to promise	versprechen
to apologize	sich entschuldigen
wing	Flügel

A mother mouse and her baby were walking in a cave when a bat flew by.
The baby mouse said, "Look, mum, *is* that an angel?"

cave	Höhle
bat	Fledermaus

To be pleased as Punch – Sich wie ein Schneekönig freuen

A male hyena brought some food home to his mate and said, "*Don't* you ever take anything seriously?"

| hyena | Hyäne |
| mate | Männchen bzw. Weibchen |

A customer walked down the row of birds for sale in a pet shop. Passing one macaw, he heard the bird speak. The customer said, "Hey, *can* you speak, stupid?"
The bird replied, "You bet. *Can* you fly, dummy?"

| customer | Kunde |
| macaw | Ara |

A lobster walked into a restaurant and sat down at a table by the window. "What would you like, sir?" the waiter asked.
The lobster answered, "*A little* mayonnaise!"

| lobster | Hummer |
| waiter | Kellner |

In the middle of nowhere
Wo sich Fuchs und Hase Gute Nacht sagen

At five in the evening, visitors to the zoo go home.
Watching them move off, the *head* ape said to the *little*
apes, "I think they feed them *now*. We'll return in the
morning!"

visitor	**Besucher**
ape	**Affe**

The mother mouse said to her daughter, "Go ahead and
marry that rat *if* you want to live in a hole for the rest of
your life!"

To feel on top of the world – Munter sein

Three men and a dog were playing bridge. A surprised man commented on the *extraordinary* performance of the dog. "He's not so *smart*," the dog's partner said. "*Every* time he gets a *good* hand he wags his tail and gives it *away*!"

bridge	engl. Kartenspiel
to comment	eine Bemerkung machen
extraordinary	außergewöhnlich
performance	Aufführung, Vorstellung
smart	schlau
to wag	wedeln

Two explorers were going through the jungle when a lion appeared on the path in front of them. "Keep calm," said the first explorer. "Do you remember what we read in that book on wild animals? *If* you stand absolutely still and look a lion straight in the eye, he will turn and run away." The second explorer said, "Fine. You've read the book. I've read the book. But has he read the book?"

explorer	Forscher
jungle	Urwald
calm	ruhig

Dog in the manger – Spielverderber

straight in the eye   gerade in die Augen

My neighbour has a dog and says, "In *some* ways he's better than a wife. The licence is cheaper, he doesn't have visiting relatives, and he already comes with a fur coat!"

licence	**Urkunde**
a relative	**ein Verwandter**
fur coat	**Pelzmantel**

Why does the hummingbird hum? Because he can't remember the words!

hummingbird   Kolibri

Two dogs met on the street and had a talk. "I feel *bad*," said one. "I think I'm heading for a *nervous* breakdown."
The *other* dog said, "Why don't you see a psychiatrist?"
The *first* dog said, "I can't. I'm not allowed on the couch!"

nervous breakdown	**Nervenzusammenbruch**
psychiatrist	**Psychiater**
couch	**Sofa (Wortspiel!)**

The real McCoy – Der wahre Jakob

A well-known actor comes *into* a bar with a gorilla and orders two martinis. The barman says *to* the actor, "Okay, what can he do, sing? Tell jokes? Dance? Act? What?"
The actor said, "Nothing."
The barman said, "Then why did you bring him *into* this bar?"
The actor said, "He's my agent!"

agent   **Künstleragent**

If you're thinking of having an animal over for dinner, a cow eats seven times as *much* as a sheep!

Two fleas were talking. One said, "*Did* I tell you I'm saving up for my own dog?"

flea   **Floh**

To wear one's heart on one's sleeve
Das Herz auf der Zunge haben

Berufe

The new patient said, "I feel like a new man."
The psychiatrist said, "*Can* this new guy afford me?"

psychiatrist   Psychiater

The average executive will jog ten minutes in order to
exercise and then take the elevator *to* the second floor!

executive   leitender Angestellter
elevator   Fahrstuhl

A writer ran into an *astute* critic one afternoon and they sat
down for a cup of coffee. The writer said, "I can't
understand it - I'm a *big* seller now, yet my work isn't
nearly as *good* as it was in the beginning."
The critic answered, "Your work is just as good as it *ever*
was. Your taste is getting *better*!"

astute   scharfsinnig

Even a worm will turn
Es geschehen noch Zeichen und Wunder

Author: "I *once* got ten pounds a word."
Friend: "How was that?"
Author: "I talked back to the judge!"

to talk back to someone	jemandem widersprechen
judge	Richter

A man sat in a doctor's office and kept up a *strange* litany: "I hope I'm *sick*. I hope I'm *sick*."
Another waiting patient asked, "Why do you want to be *sick*?"
The man said, "I'd hate to be *well* and feel like this!"

litany	Litanei

One actor has an agent *with* branches overseas. Now the actor *is out of* work *in* sixteen countries.

actor	Schauspieler
agent	Künstleragent
branch	Zweigstelle

To throw the book at someone
Jemanden nach allen Regeln der Kunst fertig machen

The doctor tried to be reassuring, "Don't worry," he said.
"*Many* people talk to themselves."
The patient said, "I know, but I'm such a bore!"

to reassure	beruhigen
a bore	ein Langweiler

A doctor, a dentist, and a lawyer were in a boat together
when a wave came along and washed them overboard.
Unable to get back into the boat, they decided two would
hold on and the third would swim to the shore for help.
The doctor volunteered.
The dentist said, "There are hundreds of sharks between
here and the land. You'll get killed."
Without *further* discussion, the lawyer took off. As he swam
towards the shore, the sharks moved *aside.* The dentist said,
"That's a miracle!"
The doctor said, "That's *professional* courtesy!"

shore	Ufer
to volunteer	sich freiwillig melden
shark	Hai
miracle	Wunder
professional courtesy	Höflichkeit unter Kollegen

You can't teach an old dog new tricks
Was Hänschen nicht lernt, lernt Hans nimmermehr

The patient said to the psychiatrist, "When you say I should forget the past, *does* that include the money I owe you?"

psychiatrist   Psychiater

The psychiatrist waited until the patient became comfortable on the couch, then said, "*Why* don't you start at the beginning?"
The patient said, "Okay. In the beginning I created the heavens and the earth ..."

psychiatrist   Psychiater
comfortable   gemütlich, bequem

The teacher asked, "*If* you had five apples and I asked for one, how many would you have left?"
A boy answered, "Five!"

To take the mickey out of someone
Jemanden auf den Arm nehmen

Something terrible happened to a magician while he was performing the trick of sawing his female assistant in half. She left the show and moved to London and Bristol!

magician	**Zauberer**
to perform	**aufführen**
to saw	**sägen**

A patient says, "I think I'm an umbrella."
The psychiatrist says, "A cure is possible if you'll open up."
The patient says, "*Why? Is* it raining?"

umbrella	**Regenschirm**
psychiatrist	**Psychiater**
cure	**Heilung**

A neurotic builds castles *in* the air. A psychotic lives *in* the castle. The psychiatrist collects rent *from* both *of* them!

neurotic	**Neurotiker**
psychotic	**Psychotiker**

It's a case of dog eat dog – Es ist ein Kampf aller gegen alle

An artist stops painting for a moment, gapes at his nude model, and starts to hug and kiss her. Flushed, he says, "You're the first model I ever kissed."
"How *many* models have you had?"
"Three. Some flowers, a plate of fruit, and you!"

artist	Künstler
to gape	starren
flushed	gerötet

The doctor examined a woman and said, "You're *anaemic.*"
She said, "I'd like a *second* opinion."
The doctor said, "You're *ugly* too!"

anaemic	blutarm
opinion	Meinung
ugly	hässlich

"Doctor, my arm got broken *in* two places."
"Don't go *back* to either *of* them!"

To beat about the bush
Um den heißen Brei herumschleichen

"Did you have a good time *at* the dentist?"
"It was a scream!"

| a scream | ein Schrei (umgangssprachlich), toll (Wortspiel!) |

It was dinnertime. One astronaut took his packaged meal and started through the escape door. The other astronaut asked *inquisitively*, "Where are you going?"
The first astronaut answered, "I'm going to eat out!"

packaged meal	Essenspackung
escape door	Rettungstür
inquisitively	neugierig

"What do you think of my painting?"
"It could be *worse*."
"I resent that."
"Okay, it couldn't be *worse*."

| to resent | übel nehmen |

No dice – Ist nicht drin

The absent-minded professor and his wife are eating dinner. The wife asks, "*Will* you pass the salt?" The professor answers, "*How* fast is it going?"

absent-minded	geistesabwesend
to pass	hinüberreichen, überholen (Wortspiel!)

A farmer went through a terrible tornado. His insurance agent asked, "Is there *much* damage to the house and to the barn?"
The farmer said, "I don't know. I haven't found them yet!"

insurance agent	Versicherungsagent
barn	Scheune

To keep a stiff upper lip – Haltung bewahren

Doctor: You should *probably* live to be eighty.
Patient: "I'm eighty-five."
Doctor: "See - what did I tell you!"

The patient came into the doctor's office, suffering from amnesia. The doctor asked, "*Have* you ever had it before?"

to suffer	leiden
amnesia	Gedächtnisschwund

The convention of scientists was being held in Las Vegas. At the dice table, Dr. Prather, an astronomer, was *happily* throwing his money around. A colleague whispered to another, "Prather is gambling as if there were no tomorrow."
The second colleague said, "Maybe he knows something!"

convention	Tagung
scientist	Wissenschaftler
dice-table	Würfeltisch
to gamble	spielen (Glücksspiel)

Beauty lies in the eye of the beholder
Schön ist, was gefällt

An actor was known as a great dresser. His suits were handmade and of the finest fabrics. Unfortunately, he never paid his tailor. One of the tailor's friends had the suspicion that the actor was completely broke.

The tailor answered, "He must have *some* money. Look at the way he dresses!"

actor	**Schauspieler**
fabric	**Stoff**
tailor	**Schneider**
suspicion	**Verdacht**
broke	**pleite**

A surgeon liked to have his patients up and about as fast as possible. On the eve of an operation, he told one patient, "Ten minutes after the operation, I'll put you on your feet. Twenty minutes after the surgery, you'll walk around the room. In half an hour, you'll walk around the entire floor." The patient said, "Doctor, will it be okay *if* I lie down for the operation?"

To back the wrong horse – Aufs falsche Pferd setzen

The doctor was *busy*, and it took hours to check all his patients. Down to Mr. Smith, the doctor apologized to the *old* man, saying, "I hope you didn't mind waiting *so long*." Mr. Smith said, "It's *sad* you couldn't see my illness in its *early* stages!"

to apologize	sich entschuldigen
stage	Stadium

The absent-minded professor is about to leave the house. His wife asks him, "*Are* you sure you've forgotten everything?"

absent-minded	geistesabwesend

Two young astronauts were discussing the space programme. One says, "Why do we have to go to the moon or Mars? Why don't we go straight to the sun?"
The other astronaut says, "*If* we come within ten million miles of the sun, we'll burn up." "So we'll go at night!"

to discuss	bereden, diskutieren

The heart of the matter – Der Kern der Sache

The tower called the pilot of a flight and asked, "*What* is your height and position?"
The pilot answered, "I'm six feet one and currently I'm in the cockpit."

currently   **derzeit**

I'm beginning to question my butcher's accuracy. The other day a fly landed on his scale. It weighed four pounds and *a few* ounces!

accuracy   **Genauigkeit**
scale   **Waage**

A policeman stopped a drunk and asked, "*Where* do you think you're going?"
"Home. I just left a New Year's party."
"New Year was a month ago."
"That's why I thought I'd better head home!"

a drunk   **ein Betrunkener**
New Year   **Neujahr**

To lie in one's teeth
Das Blaue vom Himmel herunterlügen

A diplomat is a man who can tell you to go to hell so *tactfully* that you look forward to the trip!

tactfully   taktvoll

A man went to his doctor, who gave him six months to live. The man was unable to pay the bill, so the doctor gave him *some* more months.

A lawyer was walking *down* a street and saw two cars smash *into* one another. Rushing *over*, he said, "I saw everything and I'll take either side!"

To cock a snook – Eine lange Nase machen

The patient said to the psychiatrist, "I'm so *unhappy*. Nobody takes me *seriously*."
The psychiatrist said, "No kidding?"

psychiatrist	Psychiater
serious	ernst
no kidding?	(umgangssprachlich) im Ernst?

Somebody asked a professor how science helped the business world. The professor replied, "*What* would the belt business be without the law of gravity?"

science	Wissenschaft
business world	Geschäftswelt
belt	Gürtel
law of gravity	Gesetz der Schwerkraft

"Doctor, there's a ringing *in* my ears."
"Don't answer it!"

a ringing	ein Klingeln

Everything is going haywire – Alles ist drunter und drüber

A *good* politician fulfils his campaign promises, no matter
how *crooked* he has to be to do it!

campaign promises	Wahlversprechen
crooked	unehrlich

A passenger got into a taxi and said, "Take me *any* place."
The driver said, "I'm not going that way!"

A writer bragged *about* his brilliance, saying, "I believe I'm
a writer *for* the ages."
Another writer nearby said, "Yes. Ages six *to* ten!"

to brag	angeben
ages	Ewigkeiten, Alter (Wortspiel!)

To see how the wind blows – Sehen, wie der Hase läuft

An actor walked into a *shabby* restaurant for a *quick* meal. He noticed a fellow actor cleaning the tables. Stunned, he said, "Oh dear, a man with your talent is working in this *greasy* hole?"
The other actor retorted, "At least I don't eat *here*!"

shabby	schäbig
stunned	erstaunt
greasy	schmierig
to retort	entgegnen

"Doctor, I just can't stop believing I'm a dog."
"*How* long has this been going on?"
"Since I was a puppy!"

puppy	Welpe

If work is so *terrific*, how come they have to pay you to do it?

terrific	klasse

As sound as a bell – Kerngesund

A dentist met a patient who owed him *some* money. The patient was angry because the dentist kept dunning him. Listening for a moment, the dentist finally said, "Don't gnash my teeth at me!"

dentist	**Zahnarzt**
to dun	**mahnen**
to gnash one's teeth	**mit den Zähnen knirschen**

"Doctor, you have to help me."
"What's your problem?"
"I have *some* pennies stuck in my ear."
"How long have they been there?"
"A year."
"Why didn't you come in sooner?"
"I didn't need the money!"

To be over the moon – Überglücklich sein

An artist was weary of working, so when his model showed up for the day, he said, "Will it be okay with you *if* we merely have a glass of wine and talk?"
As they sipped their wine, the artist heard a car arriving outside. He jumped up and said, "It's my wife! Quick, take off your clothes!"

artist	**Künstler**
weary	**müde**

A diplomat is a man who can convince his wife that she looks *fat* in a mink coat or that she looks *vulgar* with diamonds.

to convince	**überzeugen**
mink coat	**Nerzmantel**
vulgar	**ordinär**

A patient described the pain in his arm. The doctor asked, "*Did* you ever have this before?" The man said, "Yes." The doctor said, "Well, you've got it again!"

Hell for leather – Was das Zeug hält

"I shot my dog last night."
"*Was* he mad?"
"He wasn't too thrilled about it!"

mad	**verrückt, sauer (Wortspiel!)**
thrilled	**begeistert**

A man buys a horse *from* an advertisement saying that the horse is a fine animal. Angrily, the man returns it to the trader. "The horse you sold me is nearly blind." The trader says, "The advertisement said he was a fine horse. It didn't say he saw too well."

advertisement	**Anzeige**
trader	**Händler**

Two camels were taking a stroll *in* Cairo. One said to the other, "I don't care what people say. I'm thirsty!"

a stroll	**ein Spaziergang**
to care	**sich kümmern (um)**

To show one's true colours – Sein wahres Gesicht zeigen

Arbeit

The boss called in a young employee and said, "I'm going to mix business with a *little* pleasure. You're fired!"

employee	**Angestellter**
fired	**entlassen**

The boss was explaining the facts of business life to a new employee. "*If* you want to succeed in business, you'll need two things - honesty and smartness."
"What's honesty?"
"The truth. Keep your word when you've given it."
"What is smartness?"
"Never give your word!"

employee	**Angestellter**
to succeed	**erfolgreich sein**

A storm in a teacup – Ein Sturm im Wasserglas

Why study? The more we know, the more we forget. The more we forget, the less we know. The less we know, the less we forget. The less we forget, the more we know. *Why* study?

"The wheel was invented in Egypt. But *unfortunately* it was *square.* The slaves had *enormous* trouble pulling those carts. So the inventors sat down and *finally* came up with something."
"I know. They invented the *round* wheel."
"No. They came up with the whip. You should have seen those carts move!"

to invent	**erfinden**
cart	**Wagen**
whip	**Peitsche**

Never put off until tomorrow what you can put off until *any* time later.

to put something off until ... **etwas aufschieben bis ...**

To send someone to kingdom come
Jemanden ins Jenseits befördern

He was a responsible worker. *If* anything went wrong, they said he would be responsible for it!

responsible   **verantwortungsvoll,**
              verantwortlich (Wortspiel!)

A young pupil asked the teacher, "*What* did I learn today?"
The teacher said, "That's an odd question."
The young pupil said, "Yes, but they'll ask me when I get home!"

odd   **merkwürdig**

A man was fired by his employer. Another employee asked, "When do you plan to fill the vacancy?"
The employer answered, "He didn't leave *any*!"

fired   **entlassen**
employer   **Arbeitgeber**
employee   **Angestellter**
vacancy   **offene Stelle**

Tongue in cheek – Witzelnd

"Please don't tell *any* of your colleagues what I'm paying you on this new job."
"I won't. I'm as ashamed of my salary as you are!"

colleague	Kollege
ashamed	beschämt
salary	Gehalt

The *only* man who *ever* got his work done by Friday was Robinson Crusoe!

by	bis, durch (Wortspiel!)

A man fills out an application *in order* to get a job and does well until he gets *to* the last question, "Who should we notify *in case of* an accident?" He thinks about it and then writes down, "Anybody *in* sight!"

application	Bewerbung
to notify	benachrichtigen
in sight	in Sichtweite

To be a millstone round the neck – Ein Klotz am Bein sein

They said things wouldn't get *better* until we worked *harder*. So we worked *harder,* and they were right - things didn't get *better*!

They've finally come up with the perfect office computer. *If* it makes a mistake, it will blame another computer.

The office computer system was *down*. After working on it for hours, the repairman came up with the answer: the *big* computer was shoving all the work off onto the *little* computer!

To feel in the pink – Sich bestens fühlen

My brother is a *steady* worker. He hasn't missed a coffee break in twelve years!

steady	**zuverlässig**
coffee break	**Kaffeepause**

A young man applying for a position refused to show his references to the personnel manager. "*Why* not?" asked the personnel manager.
The young man said, "They don't do me justice!"

to apply for sth.	**sich bewerben**
to refuse	**sich weigern**
reference	**Zeugnis**
personnel manager	**Personalchef**
to do justice to s.o.	**jemandem gerecht werden**

Yesterday my boss fired me. I started to cry. He said, "I can't watch a *grown* man cry." So he took off his glasses.

to fire someone	**jemanden entlassen**

Nothing new under the sun – Alles schon dagewesen

"I work like a beaver."
"*Why*? *Who* needs dams?"

beaver	**Biber**
dam	**Damm**

A secretary said to a co-worker, "I finally got my boss to laugh out loud."
"Did you tell him a joke?"
"No, I asked for a *little* more money!"

He's got a problem *at* work. He doesn't do anything, so he doesn't know when he's finished.

To set the world on fire – Die Welt erschüttern

"I lost ten thousand two months ago. Last month I lost fifteen thousand."
"*Why* don't you close up your shop?"
"*How* would I make a living?"

to make one's living   den Lebensunterhalt verdienen

Hard work never killed *anybody*. But then, relaxing is responsible for very *few* casualties.

responsible   verantwortlich
casualty   Verletzter

A man showed up late for work. His boss said, "*What* happened?"
The man said, "The clock woke everybody but me."
"*How* could that happen?"
"Well, it was set for seven, and there are eight of us in the house!"

for   auf, für (Wortspiel!)

Every dog has his day – Jeder hat einmal Glück

A boss tried to help one of his employees improve his ways by telling him, "You have one *bad* habit. You *never* listen when people are talking to you. You get a *faraway* look and your mind wanders off. Promise me you'll work on that." The employee responded, "What was that you were saying?"

employee	**Angestellter**
faraway	**verträumt**
to promise	**versprechen**
to respond	**antworten**

Many employers nowadays look for twenty-one-year-old workers with thirty years' experience.

employer	**Arbeitgeber**
experience	**Erfahrung**

If you want to make a living, you will have to work for it. *If* you want to become rich, you will have to find another way!

To put all one's eggs in one basket
Alles auf eine Karte setzen

The *angry* boss told the *young* office-worker, "I think you're the *laziest* person I ever met. I don't believe you do an hour of work in a week. Tell me one *single* way in which the firm benefits from having you *here*."

The *young* man said, "Well, when I go on holidays, you don't have to hire anyone to take my place, and the others don't have to do any *extra* work!"

lazy	**faul**
to benefit	**profitieren**
to hire	**einstellen**

A dark horse – Eine unbekannte Größe

Essen

A customer told a slow waitress that her service was miserable.
The waitress said, "How do you know? You haven't had *any* yet!"

customer	**Kunde**
waitress	**Kellnerin**

We were *at* an art gallery where an artist with a one-track mind was showing his work. All the paintings were depictions *of* plates *of* food. We approached one *of* them showing a huge bowl *of* soup. A viewer already *in front of* the painting, obviously a fan, said, "Isn't that magnificent?" My wife said, "It needs salt!"

artist	**Künstler**
with a one-track mind	**mit nur einem Thema im Kopf**
depiction	**Darstellung**
to approach sth.	**auf etwas zugehen**
huge	**riesig**
viewer	**Betrachter**
magnificent	**großartig**

To be a pain in the neck – Auf die Nerven gehen

A diner told his *frantic* waiter, "You know, I *first* came into this place in 1938."
The waiter said, "I've *only* got two hands. I'll get to your table in a minute!"

frantic	**verzweifelt**
waiter	**Kellner**

A man applied for a position with a *large* food chain. Asked for his experience, he replied, "I eat *every* day!"

to apply for a position	**sich auf eine Stelle bewerben**
experience	**Erfahrung**
to reply	**antworten**

A guest yelled at the waiter, "*What's* this fly doing in my soup?"
The waiter said, "It's probably cooling off. It gets very hot in the kitchen!"

to yell	**schreien**
waiter	**Kellner**

Hell's bells – Heiliger Strohsack

Doctors will tell you that *if* you eat slowly, you will eat less. It is particularly true if you're a member of a large family!

particularly   **besonders**

"*Is* my face clean enough to eat with?"
"Yes, but you'd better use your hands!"

My wife is making a fortune with her cooking. Indians come *from* the Amazon to dip their arrows *in* it!

a fortune   **ein Vermögen**
to dip   **eintunken**

"Waiter, I'd like *some* chicken. The younger the better."
"Good, I'll bring you an egg!"

waiter   **Kellner**

To put one's nose to the grindstone – Ranklotzen

A *young* boy bit into an apple, saw a worm, and handed the apple to his *little* brother, saying, "I think I'll be a vegetarian from *now* on!"

A woman in a supermarket picked up a tomato, squeezed it ten different ways, then asked the produce man, "How *much* do you want for this rotten tomato?"

to squeeze	**quetschen**
produce man	**Angestellter der Gemüseabteilung**
rotten	**verdorben**

The customer said, "I want *some* oysters, but they mustn't be too big or too tough or too old, and they should be sweet and I want them right away."
The waiter said, "Would you like them with or without pearls?"

oyster	**Auster**
pearl	**Perle**

In the twinkling of an eye – Im Handumdrehen

I ordered a *complete* meal in French the *other* night, and the waiter was surprised. It was a Chinese restaurant!

| waiter | Kellner |
| surprised | erstaunt |

The waiter placed the finger bowls *in front of* the two men. Because they were unfamiliar with fine dining, one *of* the men asked, "What are these for?"
The waiter said, "You wash your hands *in* them."
The second diner said, "See? You ask a foolish question, you get a foolish answer!"

| finger bowl | Fingerschale |
| foolish | töricht |

There's a simple rule to be followed when reading menus in fancy French restaurants: *If* you can't pronounce it, you will not be able to afford it!

| fancy | schick |

To move heaven and earth
Himmel und Hölle in Bewegung setzen

Witze

Two travellers stopped at a roadside restaurant. When the waiter came over, one man said, "I'd like some coffee with milk and sugar."

The second man said, "I'd like the same, but could you make sure that the cup is clean?"

The waiter returned a *few* minutes later with their orders and asked, "All right, which one of you gets the clean cup?"

traveller	Reisender
waiter	Kellner
order	Bestellung

Straight from the horse's mouth – Aus berufenem Munde

Ninety percent of accidents occur in the kitchen. And my wife cooked quite *a few* of them!

accident	**Unfall**
to occur	**stattfinden**

"The food in this restaurant is *rubbish*."
"I know, and such *small* portions!"

"Doctor, *are* papayas healthy?"
"I never heard one complain!"

healthy	**gesund (Wortspiel!)**
to complain	**sich beschweren**

The two biggest sellers in *any* bookshop are the cookbooks and the diet books. The cookbooks tell you how to prepare the food, and the diet books tell you how not to eat *any of* it!

To drive someone crazy – Jemanden auf die Palme bringen

He knows when there's salad for dinner - he doesn't smell *any* food burning!

"Here's your coffee, sir. It's Brazilian."
"Oh, *is* that where you've been all this time?"

Every night, my wife calls me *to* dinner *with* the same sentence. She yells out, "Dinner's *on* the table. Come and guess it!"

A white lie – Eine fromme Lüge

The campaign to get people to stop smoking isn't all good. *Some* of the people got their taste buds back and realized they've been eating things for years which they absolutely hate!

taste buds	**Geschmacksknospen**
to realize	**erkennen**

I broke my dog *of* the bad habit *of* begging *for* food at the table. I let it taste my wife's cooking!

I go to a restaurant *near* the place I live that has the *worst* service. Sometimes I have to wait an hour to be served. I don't mind. The food is *awful*!

awful	**schrecklich**

A *clean* tie will always attract the soup of the day.

To hit the roof – An die Decke gehen

An inspector walks into a restaurant and says to the boss,
"You have too *many* roaches in here."
The owner says, "How *many* am I allowed?"

roach   **Schabe**
to be allowed   **berechtigt sein**

"Why do you tell people you married your wife *because of*
her great cooking?"
"I had to give some excuse!"

excuse   **Ausrede**

"*Will* you join me in a bowl of soup?"
"*Is* there enough room for both of us?"

She: "How do you like the potato salad?"
He: "It's great. It tastes almost as if you bought it yourself!"

The works – Alles Drum und Dran

The husband told his wife he wanted to be surprised *for* dinner, so she removed all the labels *from* the cans!

surprised	überrascht
to remove	entfernen
label	Etikett
can	Dose, Büchse

To have a king-sized headache
· Einen Brummschädel haben

Freizeit und Diverses

A woman whose husband had recently made a fortune bought him a *huge* yacht. Writing out a check for the amount, she told the salesman, "Make *sure* to wrap it up *well* so that he won't be able to guess what it is!"

Two ladies were relaxing at the pool. One suggested, "How about a cocktail *before* dinner?"
The other said, "No, thanks, I never drink."
The friend said, "Why not?"
"Well, *in front of* my children, I don't think it's right, and when I'm away *from* my children - who needs it?"

to suggest   **vorschlagen**

Someone who always bounces back
Ein Stehaufmännchen

"*Why* are you lying down? Are you tired?"
"I'm lying down so I don't get tired!"

"You can't say I made *any* noise when I came in last night."
"You were quiet. But the men who carried you in were noisy!"

noise   Geräusch(e), Lärm

Mrs. Dell was bragging *about* her recent trip. "Money was no object *with* us, you can see. We went *to* Italy for a month."
Mrs. Rivetti said, "So? I was born there!"

to brag   angeben

Studies show that having a pet is *good* for your health. A dog keeps the doctor *away, especially* if it's a *big* dog!

To make no bones about something – Etwas offen sagen

Karate makes sense. If you practice breaking boards in half, you'll be able to protect yourself the next time a board attacks you!

A plane with engine trouble flew *over* the Neapolitan coast. The pilot went *on* the intercom and said, "Ladies and gentlemen, you have all heard the expression 'See Naples and die.' I would suggest you look *out of* the window!"

coast	**Küste**
intercom	**Sprechanlage**
to suggest	**vorschlagen**

A man had been reading the life and death statistics put out by the government and said to his friend nearby, "*Do* you know that a man dies every time I take a breath?"
The friend said, "Try a breath mint!"

statistics	**Statistiken**
government	**Regierung**
breath mint	**Minzbonbon**

Beauty is only skin-deep – Der äußere Schein kann trügen

The *lazy* man cries, "Everything gets *easier* with practice, except getting up in the morning!"

lazy   **faul**
practice   **Übung**
except   **außer**

A drunk walked *over* to a man and asked, "Do you have the time?"
The man said, "Eight-fifteen."
The drunk said, "I think I'm going crazy. All day long I've been getting different answers!"

The quizmaster asked the contestant, "*What's* the first thing you'll do with this ten thousand?"
The contestant said, "Count it!"

To thank one's lucky stars – Glück gehabt haben

Silence is *good* because you *never* have to explain something you didn't say.

silence   **Schweigen, Stille**

"That book has a *great* ending."
"What about the beginning?"
"I didn't get to that yet!"

A man *on* a trip goes *to* the barber *of* a small town *for* a shave. After being cut several times, the man asks, "Excuse me, do you happen to have another razor?"
The barber says, "Certainly. Would you like to do your own shaving?"
"No, I'd like to defend myself!"

barber	**Friseur**
a shave	**eine Rasur**
several times	**einige Male**
razor	**Rasiermesser**
to defend	**verteidigen**

Money talks – Mit Geld geht alles

A man returned to work after his holiday, and his friend asked, "*How* did you like your trip?"
The man said, "*Did* you ever spend a week in a car with those you thought you loved?"

A *real* pessimist is *never happy* unless he's *miserable*!

miserable   **unglücklich**

To have an eye to the main chance
Auf den Vorteil bedacht sein

Success is *relative*. The more success, the more relatives!

relative   **relativ**
a relative   **Verwandter (Wortspiel!)**

The owner of a bar came home and, just as he put on the coffee, heard the phone ring. He answered it to hear a drunken voice at the other end saying, "*What* time do you plan to open your bar?"
The owner answered sharply, "I just closed. I'll open again at noon tomorrow!"
With that, he hung up. The phone rang again. The same person was at the other end. "*What* time did you say you open?"
"Noon, I told you!"
The phone rang again. "This is your old friend again. *What* time do you open?"
"I told you three times. Noon! Noon! *Why* are you so keen to get into my bar?"
The drunken voice said, "In? I just want to get out!"

to be keen (on)   **erpicht sein (auf)**
owner   **Besitzer**
keen   **stark interessiert**

Character assassination – Rufmord

I know the exact day I gave *up* jogging. It's on my birth certificate!

It was suggested that a young man improve his mind by reading. In the library he asked for a good book to read. The librarian asked if he wanted something light or heavy. The young man answered, "It doesn't matter. *If* it's heavy, I'll bring my car."

to suggest	vorschlagen
to improve	verbessern
library	Bibliothek, Bücherei

Two women met at a fancy restaurant. One asked, "Sylvia, *what* have you done to your hair? It looks like a wig." The other said, "It is a wig."
The first one said, "*Isn't* that marvellous? I never would have guessed!"

fancy	schick
wig	Perücke

To play hell with something
Etwas völlig durcheinander bringen

A customer complained, "There are so *many* fingerprints all over this glass."
The waiter said, "What other part of the body do you want it washed with?"

customer	Kunde
to complain	sich beschweren
fingerprint	Fingerabdruck
waiter	Kellner

One lady driver said it all. "The thing I hate *most* about parking is that *noisy* crash!"

To fly off the handle – Aus der Haut fahren

There's an easy way to find out the value of money - try to borrow *some*!

value   **Wert**
to borrow   **leihen**

The telephone rings.
"Hello."
"Hello, *is* this Joe?"
"This is Joe."
"It doesn't sound like Joe."
"Well, it's Joe."
"*Are* you sure?"
"Yes, I'm sure."
"Okay. Joe, this is Tom. I need two hundred Pounds."
"I'll tell Joe when he gets in."

I like jogging, *except* for the part after you put on your running shoes!

except for   **bis auf**

Give a dog a bad name – Wer einmal ins Gerede kommt

Two golfers were strolling *towards* the green when they happened to see two women *come up behind* them. One said, "Here comes my wife with some old witch she must have found *in* the clubhouse."
The other golfer said, "Mine too!"

to stroll	schlendern
witch	Hexe

He led her *closely* as they moved around the dance floor. After the fifth time he'd stepped on her toes, he said, "I can't understand it. I *never* danced so *badly* before."
"Oh," she said, "you've danced before?"

A woman rushed after the rubbish collection and asked, "*Am* I too late for the rubbish?"
The collector said, "No, jump in!"

to rush after sth.	hinter etwas her rennen
rubbish collection	Müllabfuhr
collector	Abholer

To swallow the pill – In den sauren Apfel beißen

Two drunks found themselves on a roller coaster. One said, "We're in good time, but I'll be surprised *if* this is the right bus!"

roller coaster   **Achterbahn**

A lady driver was breaking just about every rule *of* the road, and made a turn *from* the wrong lane *into* the wrong street. A policeman whistled at her. She refused to stop. The policeman finally *caught up* with her and asked, "Didn't you hear me whistle?"
The lady driver said, "When I'm driving, I don't flirt!"

to whistle   **pfeifen**
to refuse   **sich weigern**

Taking someone for a ride – Jemanden veräppeln

Holidays are easy *if* the boss will tell you when, and the wife will tell you where!

"Waiter, what's this fly doing in my soup?"
"It looks like a *little* breaststroke."

breaststroke   **Brustschwimmen**

Money doesn't make you *happy*. Is a man with eight million *happier* than a man with seven?

"*Do* boats like this sink often?"
"Only once."

The Rolls-Royce can't be *much* of a car. Very *few* people drive them!

To teach someone a lesson
Jemandem eine Lektion erteilen

A woman told another, "Last year we took a trip *around* the world. This year we're going someplace else!"

A man approached an acquaintance in a gambling casino and said, "Joe, can you give me a hundred? My wife is dying and needs a medicine that can save her. Without it she'll be dead by morning."
Joe said, "Sid, I'd give you the money right away, but I'm worried that *if* I give it to you, you'll gamble it away."
Sid answered, "No, you don't understand. Gambling money I've got!"

acquaintance	**Bekannter**
gambling casino	**Spielcasino**
to worry	**beunruhigt sein**

Last week the beach was *really* crowded. I had to dive in six times before I hit water!

crowded	**überfüllt**
to dive	**springen**

Don't judge a book by its cover
Nicht nach dem Äußeren gehen

Two men met *at* a bar and had a great evening together. They promised to meet *at* the same bar a year *from* that day. One of the men returned *at* the exact moment and found the other sitting, waiting *for* him.
"When did you get here?" the man asked.
The other said, "Who left?"

to promise   versprechen

With airline fares plummeting, it now costs as *much* to get to the airport as it does to fly somewhere!

to plummet   fallen, absacken

To ask for the moon – Etwas Unmögliches verlangen

A child was playing on the beach when a *tidal* wave came along and swept him into the water. *Ever* alert, the lifeguard dived into the water and fought the waves until he reached the child. The lifeguard held the child *securely* and swam back to the shore. The child's mother rushed to them. She kissed her *most precious* son then turned to the lifeguard and said, "Where's his hat?"

tidal wave	Flutwelle
to sweep	wegreißen
alert	wachsam
lifeguard	Rettungsschwimmer
to dive	tauchen
shore	Ufer
precious	wertvoll

The taxi arrived at the hotel. Getting out, the new bride asked her husband, "*What* can we do to hide the fact that we've just been married?"
The groom said, "You carry the luggage!"

bride	Ehefrau
to hide	verbergen
luggage	Gepäck

Charity begins at home
Man muss zuerst an seine eigene Familie denken

Once there was a man who took a holiday *in order to* forget everything. In his hotel room he opened his luggage and *found out* that he'd forgotten everything!

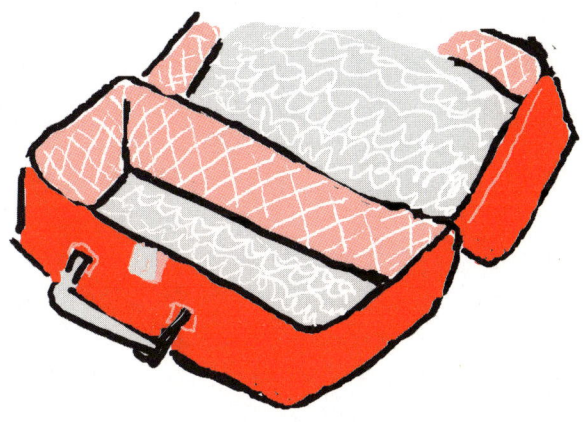

Carson, seventy-five years old, ran into his old friend Colmer. Colmer remarked that Carson looked tired. Carson said, "I just got back from Paris."
"Was it nice?"
"Paris was fine. I only wish that I'd been there *a few* years earlier."
"When Paris was Paris?"
"No, when Carson was Carson!"

to remark   bemerken

To be cheered to the echo
Rauschenden Beifall bekommen

An American couple went *to* Europe. *In* a small town *in* southern Italy, they stopped *for* breakfast. Paying *for* the meal, the husband discovered he'd been charged three dollars *for* an egg. He asked, "Is there a scarcity *of* eggs in this area?"

"No, a scarcity *of* Americans!"

to discover	**entdecken**
scarcity	**Knappheit**

Some of those new ocean liners are gigantic. Just recently on a trip, a woman came out of the elevator that brought her up to the deck and said to a crew-member, "Excuse me, but which way is the Pacific Ocean?"

ocean liner	**Ozeandampfer**
recently	**vor kurzem**
elevator	**Fahrstuhl**
crew-member	**Besatzungsmitglied**

I ruined my health by *drinking* to other people's.

To kill two birds with one stone
Zwei Fliegen mit einer Klappe schlagen

I've been drinking lots of carrot juice because it's good for my eyes. But recently I wondered *if* I'd overdone it. When I tried to sleep, I could see through my eyelids!

carrot juice	Karottensaft
recently	vor kurzem
to wonder	überlegen
eyelids	Augenlider

A boy was asked what he had been doing *during* the weekend. He explained, "*On* Sunday I went to the circus, because one *of* us children had to take dad."

"Waiter, there's a fly in my soup."
"All right, *shall* I bring you a fork?"

Where there's life there's hope
Es ist noch nicht aller Tage Abend

I stopped buying natural food when I found out that as *many* as eighty percent of people die from natural causes.

The pedestrian started to brush himself off. A man came running over to him and asked, *"Have* an accident?" The pedestrian said, "No, thanks. Just had one!"

pedestrian	**Fußgänger**
to brush sth. off	**etwas abwischen**
accident	**Unfall**

(Wortspiel mit verkürzter Frageweise: *Have sth.?* entspricht „Möchten Sie ...?" oder „Hatten Sie ...?")

The hypochondriac spent his live taking pills - iron pills, calcium pills, potassium pills - all the pills. When he died, his family had a big fight over mineral rights *to* his body!

hypochondriac	**Hypochonder**
iron	**Eisen**
potassium	**Kalium**
mineral rights	**Recht, um Minerale abzubauen**

To have the best of both worlds
Das eine tun und das andere nicht lassen

A man and his wife went on a four-day *luxury* cruise. The wife was *slightly* more than *gregarious.* In fact, she never shut her mouth. She talked at breakfast, while they were lounging on deck, at lunch, at play, and all through the night.

On the fourth morning, the man and his wife were standing on the bow of the ship when a lurch caused the wife to fall *overboard.* Seeing her bobbing up and down on the water, a crew-member ran to the husband and said, "Your wife is *overboard*!"

The husband said, "Thank God. I thought I was going *deaf*!"

luxury cruise	Luxusfahrt
gregarious	gesellig
to lounge	faulenzen
bow	Bug
lurch	Ruck
overboard	über Bord
to bob up and down	sich auf und ab bewegen
crew-member	Besatzungsmitglied
deaf	taub

I do aerobic reading. I move my lips as I *go down* a page.

One man's meat is another man's poison
Des einen Freud, des andern Leid

If you have to get *some* money, borrow from a pessimist.
He doesn't expect to get it back!

to borrow	**leihen**
to expect	**erwarten**

Money may not buy you happiness but it can make being
miserable *much* more fun!

miserable	**unglücklich**

Five dice players were in court, waiting to be arraigned.
The judge said, "*Will* the dice players come forward?" Six
men stepped to the bench. The judge said to the sixth man,
"*Why* are you up here?"
The man said, "*What's* the matter? *Isn't* my money good?"

dice player	**Würfelspieler**
to be arraigned	**angeklagt werden**
judge	**Richter**
bench	**(Anklage-)Bank**

To brush up something – Etwas auffrischen

You know that the honeymoon is *over* when the husband calls home to say that he'll *be late* for dinner and the answering machine explains that it's in the refrigerator!

honeymoon	**Flitterwochen**
answering machine	**Anrufbeantworter**
to explain	**erklären**
refrigerator	**Kühlschrank**

Not for love nor money – Nicht für Geld und gute Worte

A woman found herself *in* a valley surrounded *by* mountains. She'd say something and it would echo *back*. She went crazy trying to get *in* the last word.

valley	**Tal**
surrounded	**umringt**
crazy	**verrückt**

The relatives were visiting for the first time.
"You've got a nice place," said Aunt Bea.
Uncle Bart said, "But it looks sort of bare yet."
Cousin Jed, the host, said, "That's because we just put in the trees. I hope they'll have grown much bigger before you come here again!"

relatives	**Verwandte**
bare	**kahl**
host	**Gastgeber**

I can't believe it happened. Yesterday I jogged *backwards* and put on eight pounds!

To put one' s foot down – Ein Machtwort sprechen

In Hawaii, on a hotel door you can find a sign that asks,
"Have you left anything?"
It should ask *if* you have anything left!

to leave sth. **etwas zurücklassen**
left **übrig (Wortspiel!)**

An Englishman was showing an American *through* his
trophy room. Stopping *at* a lion, he said, "That one was
from one of father's safaris. It was stuffed *in* 1975."
"With what?" asked the American.
"Father!"

stuffed **ausgestopft**

Sue: "Are you saving *any* money since you started your
budget system?"
Helen: "Of course. By the time we have balanced it up
every night, it's too late to go anywhere!"

budget system **Haushaltsbuchführung**

Higgeldy-Piggeldy – Kuddelmuddel

Two fishermen, Al and Cal, were out on the lake *bright* and *early*. They sat *silently* as they cast for trout. Each one kept *still* so as not to frighten off any fish. After six hours, Cal shifted his feet. Al said, "What is this with you? Did you come out here to fish or to dance?"

to cast	auswerfen
trout	Forelle
to frighten	verängstigen
to shift	bewegen

A scuba diver swam slowly *from* coral reef *to* coral reef, stopping to admire the multicoloured fish and plant life. His attention was diverted *to* another diver *at* the end of a small reef. The other diver was tearing *at* the coral, huge chunks coming off *in* his hand. The scuba diver swam *over* quickly. With a small, jagged rock *from* the ocean floor he wrote *on* the side *of* the coral, "What are you doing?"
The other man *picked up* a rock and wrote, "Drowning!"

scuba diver	Taucher
coral reef	Korallenriff
diverted	abgelenkt
huge	riesig

To flog a dead horse – Offene Türen einrennen

Two hunters came across some lion tracks. One, no doubt the smarter, said, "*If you follow the tracks, you'll see where he went. I'll go back and see where he came from!*"

Come rain or shine – Was auch geschieht

Airlines are *mean*. They send your luggage to places you can't afford to go.

| luggage | Gepäck |
| to afford | sich leisten |

A woman decides to frighten her husband *out of* drinking
She dresses *up* like the devil and waits *for* him *at* the door.
As he comes *in*, she says, "Boo!"
The man says, "Who are you?"
The woman says, "I'm the devil."
The man says, "Shake hands. I married your sister!"

| to frighten | erschrecken |
| devil | Teufel |

When we arrived at the dock to board, the captain looked at my wife's luggage and said, "*If* you had told me, I would have brought a bigger ship!"

| dock | Pier, Kai |

To put one's money where one's mouth is
Taten sprechen lassen

The fakir lay on the bed of nails. As still as a dead man, he was obviously asleep. A woman tourist said to her companion, "*Can* you imagine? He doesn't even move." Her companion said, "It's a good thing. On a bed of nails you don't want to toss and turn!"

to toss and turn   sich herumwälzen

A man goes to a gypsy fortune-teller who says, "For ten pounds, I'll read your future and you can ask three questions."
"About what?"
"About anything."
"Isn't ten pounds a lot of money?"
"Not too *much.* Now, what is your last question?"

gypsy   Zigeunerin
fortune-teller   Wahrsagerin

That's the way the cookie crumbles
Das ist der Lauf der Dinge

"*Which* part of the car causes the most accidents?"
"The nut behind the steering wheel!"

accident	**Unfall**
nut	**(umgangssprachlich) Idiot**
steering wheel	**Lenkrad**

Pointing to the bear rug *on* his floor, a hunter told his friend, "I got this one *in* Canada. It was either him or me." The friend said, "Well, he makes a better rug!"

bear rug	**Bärenfell**
hunter	**Jäger**

It's *hard* to describe today's music, but yesterday I was in a restaurant where a waiter dropped a tray of dishes, and six people got up to dance.

waiter	**Kellner**
tray	**Tablett**

Do as I say not as I do
Folge meinem Rat und nicht meinen Taten

A man who'd never been to the ocean before finally went to the beach for the experience. Afraid to go into the water, he asked the lifeguard if he could bring him a bucket of sea water so that he could wet himself *a little*. Over a period of two hours, the lifeguard brought over a dozen buckets. Grateful, the man gave the lifeguard a five-pound tip. Returning the next day for more sun, the man happened to arrive at low tide. He looked at the lifeguard and said, "You've been doing a lot of business!"

lifeguard	**Rettungsschwimmer**
bucket	**Eimer**

Actions speak louder than words
Taten zählen mehr als Worte

© 1998 Weltbild Verlag GmbH, Augsburg
Alle Rechte vorbehalten

Einbandgestaltung
und Titelillustration: Thomas Uhlig, Augsburg
Illustrationen: Agentur Herwig, Bornhöved (Knut Hamann)
Layout und Satz: Agentur Herwig, Bornhöved
Belichtung: Uhl + Massopust, Aalen
Druck und Bindung: Clausen & Bosse, Leck
Printed in Germany

ISBN 3-8043-4521-2